A CUP OF COLD WATER

BEING JESUS TO THE "LEAST OF THESE"
MATTHEW 10:42

BY

CHRIS SURBER

Energion Publications
Gonzalez, FL
2016

ISBN10: 1-63199-161-2
ISBN13: 978-1-63199-161-5

Energion Publications
P. O. Box 841
Gonzalez, FL 32560

energion.com
pubs@energion.com

TABLE OF CONTENTS

TABLE OF CONTENTS

INTRODUCTION

My first mission trip to Haiti was my first mission trip any-where. For years I'd ministered to what we would call the "least of these" in America. It was meaningful ministry. I'd preached and led Bible Studies in rescue shelters and nursing homes on my off time when I was a young Marine Sergeant. Later as a pastor I've always nurtured local outreach projects and regional Christian ministry. My wife and I had written sacrificial checks to support the work of friends in Africa, India, and even Haiti. But this? I'd never per-sonally done anything like this.

My wife had gone on a trip with a group of women from a nearby church a few months earlier. God had broken her heart for Haiti specifically and for people in the world living in desperate poverty in general. As the plane flew over the capital city of Port Au Prince my heart sank. I've flown into a lot of capital cities. It looked nothing like any I had seen before. The view from the air reminded me of old "B" movie post-apocalyptic horror flicks. I wanted to go back while my wife just looked wide-eyed and said, "Isn't it beautiful …" No. It wasn't.

Even from the air you can see the poverty in tarped roofs, rubble, garbage, and a general state of disorder. Everything in me wanted to grab the pilot of the plane by the face, shake him, and say, "TURN AROUND!" It didn't get any better after we got off the plane. We were in Haiti with a marginally funded missionary. That meant riding to the city where we would be ministering that week in the back of a barely running rented pickup truck passing the sites of Third World vendors and naked bathers by the side of the road. (The city to which we headed was Montrouis near St-Marc, pronounced "Mo-Wee.")

Looking back, I was in a state of near shock. I had seen pov-erty, but nothing like this. We slept that night in the heat of the missionaries' home with electricity going in and out. I lay awake most of the night thinking about just getting through that week and wondering why I hadn't had the good sense to stay home. The next morning, we woke up early and after eating some Caribbe-

1

an bananas we headed to a dusty hill in Montrouis where God changed me forever.

On her previous trip, my Christina had met a disastrously poor little girl named Carmelie. Her parents had abandoned her long before and she lived with an elderly, Jesus-loving, desperately poor, old woman. My wife had told me about how Carmelie was so poor and hungry and always asking her for water on her previous trip, as she and the other woman on her mission team ministered in that community.

As soon as Carmelie saw us she immediately recognized Christina and ran to her, giving her a huge hug, the size of which was only matched by her immense smile. She began speaking in Haitian Creole, asking my wife for water. It hit me so hard that this was three months later and that little girl was still thirsty! Christina took her and a few dozen other kids from the community to a little make-shift classroom for a Bible lesson and singing. After they were all seated, I retrieved Carmelie and led her around to the back of a half-finished cinder block building. I took off my water-carrier backpack and poured several ounces of ice cold water into a large metal cup. I gave it to Carmelie. She drank every drop. I sent her back to the classroom to receive the Word of God. I wept.

Later I was sitting on a spare tire in the back of that rusty, barely running truck, wondering why I was so moved by that experience. Then the passage of Scripture flooded into every part of me. "And whoever gives one of these little ones even a cup of cold water because he is a disciple, truly, I say to you, he will by no means lose his reward" (Matthew 10:42). That experience was so moving because for me it was the simplest expression of Christian obedience I could recount at that time.

There was no veneer of accomplishment or title. I wasn't Pastor Surber, the former Marine Corps Staff Sergeant. I wasn't Doctor Surber the degreed minister. It was just me and a little girl and some cold water in obedience to Jesus completely out of my zone of preference and comfort. These days we use words like authentic, real, or raw to describe real Christian teaching and living. We want pastors who keep it real and we want to be believers who live authentic Christian lives but we lack biblical definitions for those terms.

Jesus is calling us into lives of simple obedience in sharing His love with the world one cup of cold water at a time, one thirsty person at a time, as we travel the highways and byways of our Jerusalem, Judea, and Samaria. Live bold for Christ like a sheep in the shadow of a mighty lion who loves us!

In the Grip of His Grace...

Pastor Chris Surber

3

I: MATTHEW 10:42 CONCISE EXPOSITION

The King has ushered in the Kingdom and now it is time for the citizens of the Kingdom to be about the work of the King. That is essentially what Matthew 10:42 is about. Kingdom citizens must to be about the work of the King. But what kind of work are we to be doing? What is the work of the King of glory in this broken world today? It is the same work that He was doing when our King's leathery sandals stirred up the dust of Galilee and stumbled up Golgotha's cruel hill carrying His Cross — compassion, truth, and redemption.

No passage of Scripture more clearly articulates this than I John 3:8. "Whoever makes a practice of sinning is of the devil, for the devil has been sinning from the beginning. The reason the Son of God appeared was to destroy the works of the devil." In this broken world, man has traded His righteous allegiance to His creator through obedience and worship, for a dastardly faithfulness to the prince of this world through sin and selfish rebellion. Consequently, rather than the law of love and compassion reigning, selfishness and destruction reign. Rather than knowing God in intimacy and truth, lies and division reign.

Jesus came to redeem humanity through His sacrificial death at the cross so that the destruction wrought in our souls for eternity could be destroyed. That is the eternal consequence of faith in Christ — believers are restored to a right relationship with their creator. The "here and now" aspect of the work of Christ in the lives of believers is that we begin to live in this world the way Jesus lived when He was in this world. God pulls us out of the insanity of serving ourselves and this world and its false king, into the sanity of relating rightly and reflecting the One who made us to be in a relationship with Him.

The central idea of Matthew 10:42 is plain obedience. Even a cup of cold water, when given in sincerity in Jesus name, conveys the compassion of Christ in undeniable simplicity. "And whoever gives one of these little ones even a cup of cold water because he is a disciple, truly, I say to you, he will by no means lose his reward."

In context, Jesus is describing the rewards of being a disciple. Jesus is saying, "Hey, if someone gives you even a cup of cold water I'm going to reward them."

Reading the rest of the chapter prior to this passage finds Jesus warning the disciples that they are going to be persecuted and reviled by men because of their allegiance to Him. Coming out of the insanity of allegiance to this fallen broken world is going to bring with it pain, but there will be rewards. Jesus is calling them "little ones" as a way of highlighting their low stature in the world, their relative poverty, their lack of possessions for having answered Jesus' call to follow Him.

Many of those God is calling us to have compassion upon today are similarly the poor disenfranchised followers of Jesus around the globe who are persecuted, either by political conditions or poverty or both. There is a direct relationship with these words of Christ and the call of the Church in our day to reach out with the basic refreshing needs of life to our brothers and sisters in chains of poverty and persecution around the world. Take note: I'm not using these two ideas interchangeably by accident. Many of our brothers and sisters in Christ around the world are persecuted by conditions of immense soul-crushing poverty within which their only hope is you and me. Don't move past this statement too quickly.

There may not be a big non-government agency coming to rescue their children from starving to death. There is likely not a government agency made up of people looking for ways to help. Somewhere in a poor village is a Christian man praying for an answer to how he is to feed his family today and the answer may very well be you.

We can also take the essence of Matthew 10:42 and apply it more broadly within the scope of other passages of Scripture that point us toward the two-fold aspect of the calling of God upon His Church: (1) Share the compassion of Christ; (2) Share the truth of Christ. It isn't just the Church that has desperate needs in this world. Through our acts of compassion it is possible to build a foundation of respect and credibility for sharing the Gospel of Christ and leading people into a repentant relationship with God in Christ.

God is calling us to share the living water of God's saving grace in Christ and the actual water that quenches a person's thirst in this dry world. Both their spirits and their bodies are dry in this arid land. If we are followers of Jesus we don't have an excuse. Everyone in the world has basic needs that need to be met and rather than waiting for somebody else to do it we need to do our part in obedience. Every natural born sinner needs the redemption that only faith in Christ offers. If we know that redemption, who are we to hoard it.

As we move forward let's consider some of the things the Bible tells us about sharing refreshing soul-saving cold water with the world with Matthew 10:42 as our stepping off point.

II: The Compassion of Christ

Jesus is compassionate. While walking the roads of Galilee, Jesus was above all things compassionate. It is God's immeasurable compassion that saves us. Were it not for compassion borne of genuine love for His creation, surely God would have left us alone in our sin or simply eradicated humanity as an imperfect sinful blight on creation. But He didn't because God is compassionate and Jesus is that very compassion for man incarnate.

In the Bible, in the gospels, the word compassion is found fourteen times. In nearly every instance it speaks directly to the character of Jesus as He shows concern and kindness to individuals, crowds, and multitudes. Here are three examples from Matthew's gospel. They give us specific insight into how we can mimic the compassion of Christ in our lives as we shine the light of the Gospel through our lives into this dark world:

• "But when he saw the multitudes, he was moved with compassion on them, because they fainted, and were scattered abroad, as sheep having no shepherd" (Matthew 9:36). They had no leadership.

• "And Jesus went forth, and saw a great multitude, and was moved with compassion toward them, and he healed their sick" (Matthew 14:14). They were sick and in need of healing.

• "Then Jesus called his disciples unto him, and said, 'I have compassion on the multitude, because they continue with me now three days, and have nothing to eat: and I will not send them away fasting, lest they faint in the way'" (Matthew 15:32). They were hungry and Jesus fed them.

Jesus showed compassion because they had no leader. God is calling us to provide godly leadership to those who are lost. At the very least this means that we should be active in sharing the Good News. In a richer fuller sense it means that we should be leading the way to wholeness in people's lives. We should be shining the light of salvation in terms of eternity and in the saving power of God to transform lives today. Get in somebody's broken life and help them pick up the pieces.

Jesus showed compassion because they were sick. Jesus showed compassion because they were hungry. It isn't enough to pray for someone who is in need or to count on somebody else, some agency, or some government office to help those in need. "But someone will say, 'You have faith and I have works.' Show me your faith apart from your works, and I will show you my faith by my works" (James 2:18). Do you believe God can change lives? Then make your faith real by being the hand of Christ in the broken life of another human in need of grace.

My friend, too often we measure our orthodoxy as Christians solely in terms of right belief. We hoard sound doctrine instead of using it as a platform for resounding Gospel living. A recommendation for a new person in our town to a "good church" often means a church with a biblical preacher. There isn't anything wrong with that but its only part of the story. A Bible preaching church should be a compassionate, reaching church.

Right belief is the foundation for right action and right action for Christians entails a lot more than writing a check to a missionary to preach the Gospel or to volunteer once a year for Vacation Bible School at your church. I'll say it again. These are good things but the life of a follower of Christ also has a lot to do with how we simply interact with the world around us in compassion to the brokenness of this world.

You've got right belief? You own the right study Bible? You pray the right prayers? You read the right books? Fantastic! Now, what about being the living breathing incarnation of the compassion of God to the people you encounter in your life? "Let us hold fast the confession of our hope without wavering, for he who promised is faithful. And let us consider how to stir up one another to love and good works" (Hebrews 10:23-24).

Right belief and right doctrine are good things but they aren't the only things! When was the last time you gave a cup of cold water to someone who was thirsty? (Matthew 10:42). Have you visited a widow or an orphan in their affliction lately? (James 1:27). Take note, I didn't ask if somebody on behalf of your church did it or if some missionary you know did it. What is currently happening in your life that fulfills those commands?

In Acts 1:8 Jesus spoke to His disciples. "But you will receive power when the Holy Spirit has come upon you, and you will be my witnesses in Jerusalem and in all Judea and Samaria, and to the end of the earth" (Acts 1:8). If we are called to pick up our cross and follow Him that means that we too are the disciples that are called to be His witnesses. If we are His witness then we must reflect the truth and compassion of Christ. It isn't enough to know or even teach the truth if we don't live it.

To preach Christ is to be Christ to those who need Christ. Our greatest instructive tool with regard to living out the compassion of Christ as followers of Christ is the example of Jesus. Sharing the compassion of Christ isn't always easy but if it takes tears to wash apathy from your eyes, so be it. If it takes a few sleepless nights to wake us up from indifference, so be it. The sacrifice of a change in perspective is a small price to pay for the beauty of seeing the world for what it really is, seeing Christ for who He really is, and seeing ourselves for who really are in the light of God's plan for our neighbor and the nations.

I sometimes feel like my soul is wandering lost when I think of all that I have seen in the eyes of the poor. I have seen the quiet desperation of mothers whose children cry to sleep in hunger. I have seen the silent resolve of those children who know nothing but such poverty and don't seek my pity. I have seen desperation turn to madness and madness become violence and rage. In all of it my heart wonders, "What's so special about a cup of cold water?" Why is Jesus calling me into their poverty with so small an offering as this? Of course, we do it because our savior commands it and He demonstrated it. But there is more to it than that. We do it because it changes lives — both ours and theirs. Most of the world suffers in poverty. Most of the world lacks stable governments. The world is really messed up.

Want to be a world-changer? It starts by realizing on a very deep assumptive level that you and I are a part of this world. We were created to create and our greatest resources are relationships! We were created to create but we can't create when we love resources more than the people for whom we were intended to co-labor in creation.

God is calling us into relationship with the hurting, broken, sinful people of this world. The Church isn't supposed to be on some other corner. It is supposed to be a present and visible light on the corners of every community. It is not contradictory to be a Bible believing soul-winning Christian and be a part of spreading the Good News of Jesus through economic development, for example. In our ministry in Haiti we do more than preach the Gospel. We do. We also create ministries that reach out to the hurting human needs of very poor people while at the same time creating employment for other poor people.

In the process we create more than economic opportunities and compassionate ministries. We create community which leads to worshipful living among the co-laborers of our ministries and the recipients of that ministry. In direct connection with local churches we are creating opportunities for Christians to be blessed and to be a blessing. You see its more than just feeling good about helping. Christ-compassion ministry provides a basis for Christians to live out their God-given mandate to be a blessing to one another, while at the same time providing a living witness in the community that the Gospel we preach produces change in our hearts. It makes our claims that Jesus changes lives visible and real.

There is something euphoric about helping the poor. There is a kind of transcendence that creeps into your psyche when you realize that without me, little old me, this person whose name I know, whose shack I've been in, whose broken sandaled feet I have walked with, without the measly five bucks I gave them, they would not have eaten today. Their son would not have gone to school this year apart from my having paid the one hundred dollar tuition for their son. There is an excitement and a joy that comes from that in your heart as you do it but we don't do it for that. We are worshipping God through service to God's people.

We love the least of these as a means of loving and worshipping Him. We worship Him through service to them in a cyclic relationship of sacrifice, service, and worship. It's not complicated. Love God and love others. Start with those lost and hurting souls in your own life and then follow God's leading to His mission field for you.

III: The Command of Christ

Jesus is Truth. Let me be very clear. Jesus gives commands and among the chief commands He has given His Church is to evangelize. That is, to spread the truth that Jesus is the truth. Becoming a Christian is becoming a follower of Christ. I'm talking about the difference between being a spectator or being an apprentice.

My family enjoys going to Colonial Williamsburg in Virginia. There you can watch men use old world methods to heat and beat steal into tools. The year my family spent living in Haiti one of the men that came to stay with us on a church mission trip happened to have been one of those blacksmiths in Williamsburg.

My son Ephram was fascinated by Nathan. He is a very kind man who took the time to show Ephram a few things about how metal works and how different rocks can make sparks and things like that. My son spent any non-working moment the team had picking Nathan's brain and enjoying time with his new friend. I watched those blacksmith hands slam huge hammers into hot iron. I was a spectator. Ephram has a friend who was a blacksmith and learned a few things from him. He took it a step further. What Jesus is commanding in us is to take several additional steps and become apprentices to the blacksmith.

Being a disciple means we do the things the Master does. We imitate Him. We gain our identity in Him. Even that only begins to describe the disciple's relationship with His Master, when that Master is Jesus. In the book of Acts, the Apostle Paul says that "In Him we live and move and have our being ..." (Acts 17:28 NKJV). Even the apprentice relationship only begins to describe the pattern of imitation prescribed for a disciple of Jesus. Our task is to love the least of these because Jesus did it and if we are in Him, and if His nature and love and life encompass the whole of our very existence, then we can't really help but be like Him and want to do the things He does.

A soccer ball can't help but bounce because it's a soccer ball. That's what it was designed and made to do. It can be flat though. It can be misshapen by years of neglect in the shade of the underbrush of the remotest part of a backyard. It can be in a forgotten corner of an attic and grow stale by years of being unused. That can happen, but as long as it's a ball its "ball-ness" remains. Regardless of where you are at in your walk with the Lord, if you are in Christ you are still in a condition that God can and will use you for His glory in your backyard, around the corner, and around the world.

What is our mission? What does it mean to live a life founded upon taking the Great Commandment seriously? The central theme of my Christian walk and of this book is this: A life of loving compassionate interaction with the world is the foundation of a life of truth-filled Gospel preaching in the world. Here is what could perhaps be called the two centrally defining passages of New Testament Scripture.

> *"Teacher, which is the great commandment in the Law?" And he said to him, "You shall love the Lord your God with all your heart and with all your soul and with all your mind. This is the great and first commandment. And a second is like it: You shall love your neighbor as yourself. On these two commandments depend all the Law and the Prophets."* – Matthew 22:36-40

> *Now the eleven disciples went to Galilee, to the mountain to which Jesus had directed them. And when they saw him they worshiped him, but some doubted. And Jesus came and said to them, "All authority in heaven and on earth has been given to me. Go therefore and make disciples of all nations, baptizing them in the name of the Father and of the Son and of the Holy Spirit, teaching them to observe all that I have commanded you. And behold, I am with you always, to the end of the age."* – Matthew 28:16-20

Passages like Matthew 10:42 find their meaning by comparing them to passages like Matthew 22:36-40. In Matthew 22 Jesus is telling His followers how to live. This is a foundational teaching of Jesus with regard to the character of our conduct in the world. In Matthew 28 He is telling His Church what to do. This is our highest purpose or endeavor. Our ultimate aim in this world is to replicate ourselves as disciples. Be and make disciples through preaching the Gospel that saves sinners and proclaiming its value in the way that you live in this broken and sinful world. The spirit of our interactions with the world, which we seek to make disciples out of, is to be one of radical love and compassion. This is what the entire book of James is dealing with.

> *Of his own will he brought us forth by the word of truth, that we should be a kind of first fruits of his creatures. Know this, my beloved brothers: let every person be quick to hear, slow to speak, slow to anger; for the anger of man does not produce the righteousness of God.* — James 1:18-20

Don't live a life of anger but of righteousness. Anger and mere moral outrage is contrary to living out the message of the Gospel. Don't settle for simple pious religious devotion. Aim for something much higher than that in your life.

> *Religion that is pure and undefiled before God, the Father, is this: to visit orphans and widows in their affliction, and to keep oneself unstained from the world.* — James 1:27

True religion is more than lighting a candle in a church. It shines the light of Christ in the world. Pure religion doesn't hoard grace for eternity. It shares it with those in need in the here and now.

> *What good is it, my brothers, if someone says he has faith but does not have works? Can that faith save him? If a brother or sister is poorly clothed and lacking in daily food, and one of you says to them, "Go in peace, be warmed and filled," without giving them the things needed for the body, what good is that? So also faith by itself, if it does not have works, is dead.* — James 2:14-17

Is there any passage of Scripture in need of less explanation and commentary? Christians are called to live in an attitude of serious love and commitment to one another and that love is to spill out to the world around. How can love this deep not splash out of the vessel of the Church onto the world?

The Great Commandment (Matthew 22:36-40) and the Great Commission (Matthew 28:16-20) are two sides of the same coin. We are commanded to bring the Gospel to all the nations. We are commanded to share the love of Christ in practical ways with the world. They cannot be divorced. They are the essence of our way. They are the spirit of a life lived reflecting Jesus in the world.

You know, the best photographers don't see objects and items. They learn to comprehend and see and capture the light reflected from objects. Great photographers look at the light not the things. Speaking on this, famed nature photographer, Ansell Adams, said, "I was climbing the long ridge west of Mt. Clark … I was suddenly arrested in the long crunching push up the ridge by an exceedingly pointed awareness of the light …. I saw more clearly than I have ever seen before or since the minute detail of the grasses, the clusters of sand shifting in the wind, the small flotsam of the forest, the motion of the high clouds streaming above the peaks. There are no words to convey the moods of those moments."

The beauty of those moments came from seeing the light differently. Our ability to be living witnesses to the power of Christ in this world similarly comes from learning to see the light differently. It comes from learning to be like the objects in those photos; reflections of His light. The emphasis in our lives must be taken off of us and placed squarely on the light bouncing off of us. We must become instruments for the reflection of His beautiful light rather than the focus and center of the picture of our lives.

Acts 1:8 is our mission. "But you will receive power when the Holy Spirit has come upon you, and you will be my witnesses in Jerusalem and in all Judea and Samaria, and to the end of the earth." Believers are witnesses locally, regionally, and unto the uttermost parts of the entire world. For believers to be effective witnesses we must be reflections of His light. We are not called to be in the spotlight but mirrors of His light. What light is coming from your life today? Is it the power of the Gospel wrapped up in acts of love and compassion — giving a cup of cold water to the least of these?

This passage tells us that our equipping power comes from the Holy Spirit. The power to fulfill the Great Commission found in Matthew 28 and the love necessary to share Christ with the world in ways in keeping with Matthew 22, Matthew 25, Matthew 10:42, and other passages that come from the Holy Spirit. Today we look for that power in all kinds of other places. Placing notable Christians in places of position isn't going to win the world to Christ or somehow "Christianize" ours or any other culture.

Amassing huge crowds and finances isn't going to create an avalanche of support for the Gospel message and turn things around in society. Political influence will never make disciples. Consider the words of Jesus immediately previous to Acts 1:8. Place Acts 1:8 in the context of the question from the disciples. "So when they had come together, they asked him, "Lord, will you at this time restore the kingdom to Israel?" He said to them, "It is not for you to know times or seasons that the Father has fixed by his own authority" (Acts 1:6-7).

Here is the resurrected Jesus standing in front of the disciples about to ascend into Heaven, on the verge of promising them power by the very presence of God taking up residence within them — and they want to know if Israel is going to regain her political independence and power! The Church today is doing the very same thing. We have the promise of power in the Holy Spirit and we're more concerned with political influence, social prominence, and shaping the morals of pagan society, than we are with walking in the power of the Holy Spirit and leading sinners into salvation through faith in Jesus Christ.

The radical power of the early Church was the ineffable power of the life lived with God. Meanwhile we would gladly trade the friendship, the intimacy, the immediate availability of the very One who created all things and is presently recreating and restoring His image in us, for smoke and lights, authority in this world, success by worldly standards, or a whole host of things other than reliance upon the Spirit of the Living God and obedience to our only true task — live as disciples and make more disciples!

The power of Pentecost — our power — is to the very presence of God in us! The Church has been given a task by God that we are not capable of accomplishing. We can never reach the world in our strength. That's why Christ promises, "You shall receive power after the Holy Spirit is come upon you." Both the Spirit of God and His power are promised. The Holy Spirit comes upon believers as an equipping power.

C.S. Lewis famously quipped that we are supernatural beings having a fleshly experience in this world. But you and I are constantly under-spiritualizing our lives. If we are filled with the Holy Spirit then we are not only to be reflections of the light of Christ, we are like light houses, with the very light of God emanating from inside of us. We are His witnesses. This brings us to the second idea contained in Acts 1:8. Our great task is to be witnesses for God. The light that people see reflected from our lives and proceeding from our hearts is the light through which they will interpret the light of Christ.

Why do we soft sell that responsibility today? If you claim Christ, you are His witness in this world in proclamation and in action — in compassion and in commission. I remember hearing another preacher tell the story of a man who received Christ in prison. Christ said to him, "I will come and live in you and we will serve this sentence together." They did. Several years later he was discharged, and just before he went out he was handed a two-page letter written by another prisoner.

It read, "You know that when I came into this jail I despised preachers, the Bible, and everything. I went to the Bible class and the preaching service because there wasn't anything else interesting to do. Then they told me you were saved, and I said, 'There's another fellow taking the gospel road to get a parole'; but, I've been watching you for two and a half years. You didn't know it, but I watched you when you were in the yard exercising, when you were working in the shop, when you played, while we were all together at meals, on the way to our cells, and all over, and now I'm a Christian, too, because I watched you. The Savior who saved you has saved me." This man read the letter and broke out in a cold sweat, thinking, "He watched me."

The world is watching. What are they seeing? When it comes to broken people in our communities, do they see compassion? When it comes to outcasts in our society, do they see that the Church is the soft place to fall? When the world looks at us do they see more than just another political demographic? We are not called by God to be witnesses to a moral agenda or a good way of life. We are supposed to be reflections of the light of Christ radiating the beauty of heaven in a dark world.

There is some fair criticism levied against ministries and movements that feed the belly without feeding the soul. However, to dismiss the call of compassion on the Church or the value of practical acts of love is to burn up the book because you don't like the forward. It is to completely ignore one whole thread of biblical teaching with regard to compassion and kindness that runs through the entire Bible. It is to abandon a primary tool for opening hearts and minds to the message of God's saving faith through in Jesus Christ.

Christianity is not another political alternative. It is a complete alternative. It is the way God's restorative power transcends everything else. This isn't another brand, it's a completely other substance. This isn't a more moral lifestyle, its entrance into life with God and that go beyond anything that can be found in this world! People no longer have to suffer in chains. They can be free in Christ! People no longer have to be afraid. They can take heart in Jesus!

A lot of Christians are saying a lot of things but neither their words, their lives, or the things they seem to care about say, "Jesus saves." We're telling angry, confused, hurt, and broken people not to infringe upon our delicate sensibilities and our moral preferences a lot more often than we are telling them and showing them that there is redeeming, healing, gentle, and kind, powerful love available in Christ and among His followers.

Our angry political shouts build a lot more walls to keep people out of the Kingdom than bridges to invite people in. God have mercy on the Church for cursing the darkness so much more than we shine the light. Evangelism isn't just words and it is more than action. The unbelieving world has a good hypocrite radar.

Our power is supernatural in the Holy Spirit. Our task is to be witnesses for God — living reflections of the light of Christ — living lighthouses. The third idea contained in this passage of Scripture is this: Jesus has given us a clear method to share His Gospel with a hurting world. The believer is to witness where he is. They were in Jerusalem. He is to move them progressively outward.

That is typified here by the context of the early Church as Judea and Samaria. We are to do so until we have a part in reaching the world.

This is a personal call for every believer. It isn't something to be "contracted out" to local outreaches, regional organizations, or foreign mission agencies. All of those things are good things but they are vehicles through which individual followers of Jesus are to engage in reaching their Jerusalem and Judea and the world. We have powerful tools! God's love in us is sure footing. God's grace exercised through kindness invites the world in. Getting smaller in the world makes us bigger for Christ. We don't need more political influence or social prominence. We need more lived grace in individual people's lives.

So how do you do it? We engage the world with the heart and the truth of Jesus Christ. It is a simple formula of loving people like Christ and leading people to the truth of Christ. The Great Commandment and the Great Commission are two tracks of the railroad of outreach and evangelism. The compassion of Christ is the evidence of the truth of Christ. There are a lot of folks who want to separate those two biblical ideas as with a razor knife. I don't know how you do that effectively in practice. People who don't do evangelism have a lot of good ideas about how others are doing it wrong.

I don't know how people can possibly stick with an "I'm only preaching the Gospel" attitude. I don't see any separation between the teachings of Christ concerning righteousness and the life of Christ concerning compassion. They are two sides of the same coin. One evening in Haiti I was walking to preach in a church and I saw a kid I knew who told me he hadn't had food in his house in weeks. I gave him money to give his mom to buy food and brought him to the revival to hear the Word of God. In practice, you do both.

IV: What Now? How Do I Do It?

I'm a pastor and a missionary. I don't want to teach anything that can't be implemented. There is nothing less useful than knowledge in a vacuum without application. Once God has awakened you to the need for every member of the Body of Christ to get personally engaged in sharing a cup of cold water with the least of these, we've got to figure out where specifically we fit into His plan to reach our communities and the nations with Christ-Compassion and the Gospel.

Here are a few of the ways we can do it:

• **Mindset:** The call to serve the least of these is a personal command for every follower of Jesus. Start thinking in terms of how you can personally participate in the plan of God for reaching the nations with the Gospel and the compassion of Christ. The mission can never happen without senders and goers.

• **Sending:** What can you do to send missionaries overseas? What can you do to support the women's shelter or the outreach mission in your community? I know a woman who decided to get her real estate license after having raised her children, so that every time she sells a home she and her husband can send money to build a home for impoverished people somewhere in the Third World.

Think bigger than only your own two hands. What can you do to mobilize your church, Sunday school class, small group, or civic organization to raise needed funds, to pray, to nurture, and to equip and empower those on the front lines? When I was a Marine serving in a tank unit, it was common knowledge that for every one infantryman, it takes several supply and support personnel. It is no different in the Church. If God isn't calling you to go, He has already called you to send.

• **Going:** There is a difference between buying a laborer a shovel and carrying a bucket of dirt. As a "goer" you begin to seek opportunities, ways, and means of getting engaged in local, regional, and foreign missions and outreach activity.

Change how you think. We've got to think differently than we've been taught to think in our culture. How dangerous it is to be a Christian in America today! If you and I really want to live differently, this is where it starts. When it comes to how we're living our lives as Christians, we don't often live as though there is much connection between what we think and what we do, at least not in any obvious or concerted way. Our actions act as litmus tests to the reality that our energy is mostly given over to pleasing ourselves or maybe to doing what we think is good for our family, our children, and our future.. In other words, most of what we do is about work and pleasure and it highlights the fact that most of our thoughts have little to do with service.

In Mark 12:30-31 Jesus says, "'You shall love the Lord your God with all your heart and with all your soul and with all your mind and with all your strength.' The second is this: 'You shall love your neighbor as yourself.' There is no other commandment greater than these." Do you see the direct connection in the words of Jesus between giving our soul, mind, and strength to loving God and the subsequent action of loving our neighbor as our self? You can't love your neighbor enough to share the compassion of Christ or the Gospel of Christ with him if we don't first fix the intentions of our soul, the direction of our mind, and the activity of our strength to loving God.

Sharing Christ outwardly with the world is the natural outcome of having been consumed by Christ inwardly. The trouble is that most of us have a dangerously low view of the importance of the message of the Cross and it causes us to keep to ourselves. More specifically we have such an unaffected heart and mind that our actions are not forced into conformity with the will of God for our lives. We're like people dressed up as soldiers for a costume party. We've got the right attire but lack the training, discipline, and power to do any soldiering.

Or we were once soldiers with training, equipping the heart for battle, but we lost our way. We became like the man spoken of by the Apostle Paul in 2 Timothy 2:3-9:

Share in suffering as a good soldier of Christ Jesus. No soldier gets entangled in civilian pursuits, since his aim is to please the one who enlisted him. An athlete is not crowned unless he competes according to the rules. It is the hard-working farmer who ought to have the first share of the crops. Think over what I say, for the Lord will give you understanding in everything. Remember Jesus Christ, risen from the dead, the offspring of David, as preached in my gospel, for which I am suffering, bound with chains as a criminal. But the word of God is not bound!

We've bound up the Word of God with our lack of willingness to live it, to shout it, to share it with the world! On the one hand we have unparalleled access to the truth of Almighty God. But then we have the unrivaled, unmitigated gall to disobey it in the name of God's love, without regard for His righteous judgment. We've made a cotton candy vendor of the Supreme Being in the universe; we've made the King a jester in His own court.

We've got to unleash our mind from the chains of complacent Christianity where we have become the mission field and the pastor is the missionary. We've got to free our thinking from all of the reasons God can't use us. We've got to shift our thinking in the direction of seeking ways to be used by God in this world and away from our need for comfort, our need for help, our problems, and getting our way. We think so much on the things of this world as they pertain to us that there isn't any room for the things God wants to do through us.

> *For those who live according to the flesh set their minds on the things of the flesh, but those who live according to the Spirit set their minds on the things of the Spirit. For to set the mind on the flesh is death, but to set the mind on the Spirit is life and peace. For the mind that is set on the flesh is hostile to God, for it does not submit to God's law; indeed, it cannot.* – Romans 8:5-7

I'm talking about complacency and apathy. I'm talking about a modern church culture within which it is easier to take up an offering for a better building we don't need, or a new parking lot to make it more convenient to come to church and feed our over nourished, underworked spirits, than it is to get people motivated about the life of sacrifice and service that Christ calls His followers into. What did Jesus say when He called the disciples? Follow me and I'll keep you safe in your nice building? I'll keep you entertained with smoke-filled glittery worship services? No.

And he said to them, "Follow me, and I will make you fishers of men" (Matthew 4:19).

Outward acts of compassion and public displays of the Gospel's power to transform lives are the very stuff that discipleship is made of. The average Christian today is about 3,000 verses overweight. Marathon runners load up on carbohydrates before a race. They pack energy into their physical bodies then they burn the energy in a grueling run. We've been doing the same thing spiritually. We're loaded up on Bible truth that we're not living out!

Listen, if it takes tears to wash apathy from your eyes, so be it. If it takes a few sleepless nights to wake us up from indifference, so be it. The sacrifice of a change in perspective is a small price to pay for the beauty of seeing the world for what it really is, seeing Christ for who He really is, and seeing ourselves for who we really are in the light of God's plan for our neighbor and the nations.

In the big picture of church culture, we are more concerned with crowds than obedience. We are more interested in entertainment and being liked by the masses than we are being in submission to God. Individually, we either want to appear to be radical without it costing us anything or we just want to have a neat, quiet little faith that gives a little comfort and tucks us into bed at night. We surely don't want the kind of Christian life that actually costs us everything or that rocks the sea of our life, upon which we sail our little sparkly ship of personal contentment, named the Headed to Happiness.

The most dangerous thing you can ever do is take Jesus seriously. If you like your life the way it is, then don't do it. If you are comfortable and want things to stay the same, take Jesus' teaching as mere metaphors and nice ideas but don't ever, ever, take Him seriously. But if you want to step off the cliff of mundane religion into the ocean of God's grace, change the way you think. There is a lot more life available for our Christian life if we'd start dying to self.

Change how you view your stuff. Was it a figure of speech when Jesus told the rich young ruler to sell everything he owned, give it to the poor, then he could be His disciple? Jesus looked at him and loved him, and said to him, "You lack one thing: go, sell all that you have and give to the poor, and you will have treasure in heaven; and come, follow me" (Mark 10:21). I've taught it that way. I've heard others teach it that way. The truth is we were both wrong. Jesus simply told that man, "Hey, sell your stuff, give it to the poor, and then you can be my disciple. Oh, and by the way, you'll be trading wealth in this passing, fleeting world for wealth in Heaven that can never pass away." He said what He said.

As one of my seminary professors used to say, "All means all. That's all 'all' means!" He said sell it all and then follow me. Now, we can principle-ize but let's not cannibalize it. For this man — and that means for some of us — Jesus is calling us to do some radical rethinking and take serious actions when it comes to how we think about and use our stuff. What stuff? I'm glad you asked. According to the driving principles of Mark 10:21 — all of it.

We cling so tightly to the stuff of this life that we seldom experience the rich deeper beauty that is available to us when we let go of this world. We are in love with houses that constantly need maintenance, cars that break down, entertainment that only lasts a few minutes, and all the while Jesus is saying, "That stuff will never satisfy the inner cravings you have for meaning. I'm offering you a better way."

That better way is to take an active inventory of how we are using our money, time, talents and possessions for Kingdom purposes. Here's a concrete example from my life. A few years ago after my wife had dragged me to Haiti and we'd made a firm commitment to moving to Haiti, I realized that I had to downsize my things. Among all the material things that I love in this world, easily chief among them are my books. At that time my personal library consisted of about four thousand books. That's a conservative estimate and not including the tens of thousands of books I own digitally through various Bible software collections.

In preparation for transition for a season in Haiti I felt the Lord compelling me to sell my books. It wasn't really a practical matter because we stored many of those books while living in Haiti. I didn't feel like He was commanding me to sell them all as much as to un-cling to them by parting with all the ones that were not essential. I tearfully sold or gave away more than two thirds of my books. Oh, was it ever difficult to do! But it's what God had for me to do as an exercise in letting go of this world.

What do you love most in this world that may be something to you like my books have at times been to me? Start there and pray for God to reveal to you the ways that our hobbies, interests, pastimes, even good work doing, may be a source of idolatry in our life. What is God saying you could do without so that you can gain more of the joy that comes from turning your stuff back into His stuff on loan to you?

Change how you view your life. This is the key. My wife Christina recently came back from leading a week-long mission team to Haiti to work and support our friends and activities there with our ministry *Supply and Multiply*. She came back from giving her life away for a week -- refreshed. A very sweet older woman in the church I pastor told me, "She just looks so beautiful after having come back from Haiti." The truth is that she looks the same. The difference is that her countenance is different. Her soul is smiling through her eyes and face.

You see, what she and I have discovered is that the more we give away from this world, the more God gives us things that really matter. The less money we have, the more joy we have because we've used God's money for things of eternal value. The less time we have, the better we sleep because we've used our life for lasting Kingdom things.

When you share a cup of cold water with the least of these, you are in turn unleashing the cool refreshing spiritual water of the Holy Spirit in your own life. That's not to say that we serve to be served. That is simply to say that when you participate in God's plan for your life in this world you step into the stream of His pure love and gain things far greater.

In Matthew 10:39 Jesus says, "Whoever finds his life will lose it, and whoever loses his life for my sake will find it." Material stuff is only as valuable as its intended purpose. If I were drowning, I'd not want a life preserver made of gold. Today, people are drowning in oceans of meandering, meaningless connections of stuff that is dragging them down. The only way to float is to let go of those heavy earthen treasures so we can swim to the shore of grace.

If you love this world, be careful about taking Jesus too seriously. When you lose your life for His sake, His promise is that you'll enter a life of sacrifice where His joy becomes your treasure. Becoming a holy water carrier to a thirsting world is dangerous, but in the danger lays opportunity. It's painful to be awake to the world's suffering, but better to be awake to the pain and find Christ's healing in it, than to be asleep to suffering, your only comfort in this world your apathy and resignation from the battle.

Fight the good fight of the faith. Take hold of the eternal life to which you were called and about which you made the good confession in the presence of many witnesses (1 Timothy 6:12).

WHAT IF?

What if, instead of a few, occasional, random acts of kindness, we started doing intentional acts of obedience? The with-God life is really a pretty simple thing. We, like Jesus, are to be the living, visible, in-flesh, incarnation of the love, beauty, power, mystery, and grace of the eternal God.

In Matthew 28 Jesus says, "All authority in heaven and on earth has been given to me. Go therefore and make disciples of all nations, baptizing them in the name of the Father and of the Son and of the Holy Spirit, teaching them to observe all that I have commanded you. And behold, I am with you always, to the end of the age" (Matthew 28:18-20).

Earlier in his gospel in Chapter 25, Matthew records Jesus saying, "For I was hungry and you gave me food, I was thirsty and you gave me drink, I was a stranger and you welcomed me, I was naked and you clothed me, I was sick and you visited me, I was in prison and you came to me.' Then the righteous will answer him, saying, 'Lord, when did we see you hungry and feed you, or thirsty and give you drink? And when did we see you a stranger and welcome you, or naked and clothe you? And when did we see you sick or in prison and visit you?' And the King will answer them, 'Truly, I say to you, as you did it to one of the least of these my brothers, you did it to me'" (Matthew 25:35-40).

Jesus commands us, His disciples, to preach the good news, the good news that He died for sinners and rose again; that He defeated death and the grave and we can have new life in Him. Jesus also tells us to feed, clothe, care for, and love the least of these. God is calling us to abandon ourselves to lives of Christ-centered compassion. When we do, the world sees Jesus on the Cross in us.

What if, He's calling us to life with a mission — and what if, we lived with a purpose. Go therefore and make disciples and as you go, be a living witness to the power of the Gospel.

What if we preached it and lived it?

What if it's simple and what if we simply lived it out?

Where people are starving, feed them. Where they are hurting, help them. All men are spiritually poor, preach the saving Gospel that saves men's souls. And in all that you do be the incarnation of Christ to a hurting broken world. **What if** …

POINTS TO PONDER

CHAPTER I: MATTHEW 10:42 CONCISE EXPOSITION

1. The author says that the work of the Church to carry the compassion, truth, and mercy of Jesus into this world today, just as Jesus did while stirring up the dust of this world during His earthly ministry.

a. How are you, your family, and your church sharing the compassion of Jesus?

b. How are you, your family, and your church sharing the truth of Jesus?

c. How are you, your family, and your church sharing the mercy of Jesus?

2. Is it possible to truly embrace the truth of the Gospel of Christ without embracing the reality of His ministry of compassion to the broken, the outcast, and the poor?

3. What does it mean to be a pilgrim in this world? If a believer is "in Christ" how ought that affect the way he or she lives in this world?

4. Should Christians in relatively comfortable situations even care about Christians suffering under political, economic, or other forms of affliction?

5. The author writes, "Somewhere in a poor village is a Christian man praying for an answer to how he is to feed his family today and the answer may very well be you."

a. What is your response to those words on an emotional level?

b. What is your response to those words on a spiritual or biblical level?

c. What shall be your response to those words on an action level?

CHAPTER II THE COMPASSION OF CHRIST

1. The author writes, "In the Bible, in the gospels, the word compassion is found fourteen times." What does the volume of discussion in the gospels concerning compassion tell us about the character of God? What does it tell us about our role in the world?

2. If Jesus was about action, is it enough for us to rest our Christian identity strictly on the possession of a right belief? Doe right beliefs about Jesus compel us to right action on behalf of Jesus? Is there a connection between biblical orthodoxy and compassion?

3. When was the last time you gave a cup of cold water to someone who was thirsty?

4. What does the Bible say about someone who professes Christ but does nothing to demonstrate the reality of that professed faith? (James 2:14-26).

5. Is there a connection to how a Christian lives and how they are received in witnessing, preaching, and telling others about Jesus?

6. What's so special about a "cup of cold water"? Does my little offering really matter? If it does, what makes it matter?

7. When you think about entering into relationships with very poor people, what comes to mind? Does it feel comfortable? What about it feels uncomfortable? Is there a way to conquer our discomfort? What role does obedience play?

CHAPTER III THE COMMAND OF CHRIST

1. What does it mean to imitate the Master as His disciple?
a. What role does identity play in being His disciple?
b. What role does obedience play in being His disciple?
c. What role does the Church play in being His disciple?

2. Can God use you regardless of your age, health, educational level, or economic status? If so, how ? If not, why not?

3. Why does God choose to use His people rather than doing everything supernaturally?

4. What is our mission? What does it mean to live a life founded upon taking the Great Commandment seriously?

5. The Great Commandment (Matthew 22:36-40) and the Great Commission (Matthew 28:16-20) are two sides of the same coin. We are commanded to bring the Gospel to all the nations. We are commanded to share the love of Christ in practical ways with the world. They cannot be divorced. They are the essence of our way. They are the spirit of a life lived reflecting Jesus in the world.

What does it mean to encounter the divine supernaturally through obedience to God through sharing the Gospel with the world? Is it possible that service to God is a means of worship and encounter with God?

6. What does it mean to depend upon the Holy Spirit in service and sharing the Gospel?

a. Do you have a personal story about the Holy Spirit empowering you to do something that you could not have done on your own?

b. What are you doing to put yourself in a position to need to trust God completely in order to gain a story like that?

7. Why do we soft sell that responsibility today. What role does simple obeience play in being a disciple of Jesus?

CHAPTER IV WHAT NOW? HOW DO I DO IT?

1. What are you doing to broaden your opportunities to share the truth of the Gospel and the compassion of Christ?

2. What are you doing to cultivate within yourself and educate others toward having a mission mindset at home and abroad?

3. What are you doing to cultivate within yourself and educate others toward having an active role in sending the Gospel and the compassion of Christ at home and abroad?

4. What are you doing to prepare to go or to equip and enable others to go?

5. The litmus tests to the reality that our energy is mostly given over to pleasing ourselves or maybe to doing what we think is good for our family, our children, and our future, most of what we do is about work and pleasure and it highlights the fact that most of our thoughts have little to do with service.

Are you prepared to seek God, even if it hurts, to share a cup of cold water?

TOPICAL LINE DRIVES

Straight to the Point in under 44 Pages

All Topical Line Drives volumes are priced at $5.99 print and $2.99 in all ebook formats.

Available

The Authorship of Hebrews: The Case for Paul	David Alan Black
What Protestants Need to Know about Roman Catholics	Robert LaRochelle
What Roman Catholics Need to Know about Protestants	Robert LaRochelle
Forgiveness: Finding Freedom from Your Past	Harvey Brown, Jr.
Process Theology: Embracing Adventure with God	Bruce Epperly
Holistic Spirituality: Life Transforming Wisdom from the Letter of James	
	Bruce Epperly
To Date or Not to Date: What the Bible Says about Pre-Marital Relationships	
	D. Kevin Brown
The Eucharist: Encounters with Jesus at the Table	Robert D. Cornwall
The Authority of Scripture in a Postmodern Age: Some Help from Karl Barth	
	Robert D. Cornwall
Pathways to Prayer	David Moffett-Moore
Rendering unto Caesar	Chris Surber
The Caregiver's Beattitudes	Robert Martin
What is Wrong with Social Justice	Elgin Hushbeck, Jr.
I'm Right and You're Wrong	Steve Kindle
Words of Woe: Alternative Lectionary Texts	Robert D. Cornwall
Why Christians Should Care about Their Jewish Roots	Nancy Petrey
Stewardship: God's Way of Recreating the World	Steve Kindle
Constructing Your Testimony	Doris Horton Murdoch
From Words of Woe to Unbelievable News	Robert D. Cornwall
Ruth and Esther: Women of Agency and Adventure	Bruce G. Epperly
Jonah: When God Changes	Bruce G. Epperly

Forthcoming

God the Creator: The Variety of Christian Views on Origins	Henry Neufeld
Textual Criticism: A Basic Guide	Thomas Hudgins

(The titles of planned volumes may change before release.)

Generous Quantity Discounts Available - Dealer Inquiries Welcome
Energion Publications — P.O. Box 841
Gonzalez, FL 32560
Website: http://energionpubs.com
Phone: (850) 525-3916

WILL YOU
JOIN THE CAUSE OF
GLOBAL MISSIONS?

DAVID ALAN BLACK
FOREWORD BY ALVIN L. REID

ALSO BY CHRIS SURBER

"What does it mean to render to Caesar what is his and render to God what is His? How a believer understands this text will, to a large degree, determine how they will approach matters of nationalism and politics as they follow Jesus."

– Dr. Chris Surber

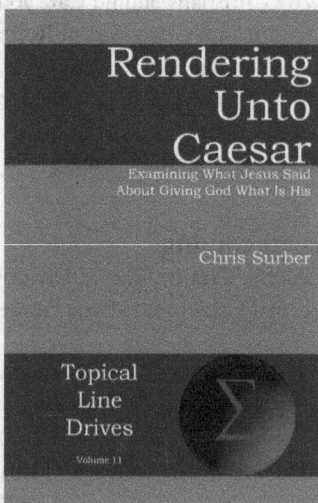

Rendering
Unto
Caesar
Examining What Jesus Said
About Giving God What Is His

Chris Surber

Topical
Line
Drives
Volume 11

www.ingramcontent.com/pod-product-compliance
Lightning Source LLC
Chambersburg PA
CBHW011750020426
42331CB00014B/3345